Praise for *Monsoon on the Fingers of God*:

"Throughout the collection, language and imagery glint off of each other, a dizzying Ferris wheel of taste, touch, and sound . . . *Monsoon on the Fingers of God* is an intricate dance between inclination and emotion, a palimpsest of migration in which several layers shine through. Along with the poet, the reader finds that their worldview has shifted, their way of looking at the world much brighter after the deluge."
—*India Currents*

"Reading Sasenarine Persaud's newest collection, *Monsoon on the Fingers of God*, is like stepping inside a clock and running a thumb along each gear and dial in order to better understand time. [...] Persaud somehow balances righteous anger with grief and heartbreak in each poem, dodging deftly from era to era to demonstrate just how closely history repeats itself. After reading this book, readers will not return to their own cities in their own present moments unchanged."
—*World Literature Today*

Praise for *Love in a Time of Technology*:

"[T]he poet's mastery of the English language is underwritten by ancestral histories and myths. Love is age-old and universal . . . Persaud is a poet of precise language, of the finely-honed meaning . . . "
—*Wasafiri*

BOOKS BY
SASENARINE PERSAUD

Mattress Makers

poetry

SASENARINE PERSAUD

MAWEN*Z*I
HOUSE

We acknowledge the support of the Canada Council for the Arts for our publishing program. We also acknowledge support from the Government of Ontario through the Ontario Arts Council, and the support of the Government of Canada through the Canada Book Fund.

Cover design by Sabrina Pignataro
Cover photo: Alfian Widiantono/Coconut fiber – stock photo/Getty Images
Author photo by Denise Noone

The following poems appeared in slightly different forms in various issues of *The Caribbean Writer*: "Waterloo: at Siewdass Sadhu's Temple in the Sea", "Puerto Rican Espousing Julia de Burgos", "Sugarcane's Black Snow", and "Mattress Makers."

"Parrot" appeared in *Trickster Tactics: A Festschrift in Honor of Peter Nazareth* (2021).

"Holi: Spring Festival of Colours" appeared in *Stabroek News*, March 2022.

"Thanksgiving" appeared in *Bostonia*, fall 2022.

Library and Archives Canada Cataloguing in Publication

Title: Mattress makers : poetry / Sasenarine Persaud.
Names: Persaud, Sasenarine, author.
Identifiers: Canadiana (print) 20230201652 | Canadiana (ebook) 20230201709 | ISBN 9781774150948 (softcover) | ISBN 9781774150955 (EPUB) | ISBN 9781774150962 (PDF)
Classification: LCC PS8581.E7495 M38 2023 | DDC C811/.54—dc23

Printed and bound in Canada by Coach House Printing

Mawenzi House Publishers Ltd.
39 Woburn Avenue (B)
Toronto, Ontario M5M 1K5
Canada
www.mawenzihouse.com

Contents

Royal Museums

Looking back through that time—
tunnel where sounds and light distort
where different bulbs exude different
hues and heat are museums for some
gleaning from that distance and this
a preoccupation with lit cobwebs
littered with unconsumed bodies

Colonial Crossing the River Tweed

Midmorning music comes in waves
again from wetlands across the street
holes appear in several spots
again asphalt poured patches
like those on punctured bicycle tubes
—a domino series—tyres balding
easier pierced, we avoided corners
where tacks and nails converged—
a green three-wheel tractor-trailer
seen nowhere else originating in Europe

What did we send? Demerara sugar
crystals purloined in Colombia or Florida
rice, bauxite extracted from sandpits
diamonds suctioned from Potaro
riverbeds and tributaries, molasses
aged rum in English oak casks—
mid-morning comes again clattering
beetles, cicadas, a thrasher on lawns
green with summer rains screaming
jays a cardinal calling mocking birds
all saying the same thing differently—
or were those pleas to enter
Untransgendered panties? Silence?

We walk across the River Tweed
not looking back or around but forward
the tiny sign in old English
script—no frills no digital board—
white stone: England England *English*

Cardinal

Late this morning rattling beaks
an automatic rifle shattering dawn
we speculated: did your alarm fail
did you oversleep in love's warmth
maybe birdflu or swinevirus—
apologizing profusely to pigs—
metamorphosing song to grunt
Om shanti shanti shanti Om

Canal No 2 Polder[*]

Bannerjee on strings derived
from Saraswatie's vina stranger
over years and time. Teenage
something loved or thought—dust
over decades Yarrow's taxi flying
red clouds' plumed wake on loam
a rocket—why did we yearn
for evenings on Savis Dam for sunsets
on tall grass for savannah inundated
vermilion and turmeric liquid
after the rains listening not with ears
or eyes or hearts even on monitors
for all we were will never be and are

[*] A village on the west bank of the Demerara River, Guyana

3

Secrets

Grass grown high is seeded
grass uncut greener in summer
rains higher than hot air balloons
rising at dawn then sinking—
gauling alighting in field—playing
games over cyberspace: I will hold
your secrets I can assure you
discretion in that ancient time
I knew your hand on paper
quink—what—ink or mount blanc
feather or this fine steel nib
what—and we could always burn
pages lost love bitter expletives
ashed, none wiser not even mail
man or memory but email is forever

Realism and Models

I would take those ankles, calves
rounded like Dutch edam
cleaved on canvas beds any night
or day—paint blobs, oils, hair
straightened on sticks, brush strokes
—before these starved matchsticks
on Paree catwalks or Manhattan's
wriggling nonexistent hips asses
flat as the world before Columbus
didn't fall off curves beyond horizons
or Isabella's forehead—neither did we

Summer Evening

Queen crape—any colour she pleases
this summer's end lilac puffs
touching green cheeks along our Drive
no Martian invasion El Nino
rains almost unceasing, king sun today
golden scepters splashing cypress
pussy willow—pig!—swallowing pines
grass in barbered diagonal strips potted
purple orchids twining heavenly bamboo
nandina's pointed leaves robellini palm
askew ceramic containers—table laid
golden rod leaves shimmering in
evening breeze myrtle—only you missing

Late Tea

1

And yet in curving jamun* twinkling
golden rod leaflets green Indian heart-
leaves bending outside our window
in Miami or Georgetown or Varanasi
starburst saijan blossoms are winter
flakes in summer dancing on hearts
southern heat confederate jasmine
battle flags' red cheeks—bells ringing
brass gifting a token from South Asia
stored out of sight yet always here
come summer's end swiftly and never

2

Film on door from green avocado clumps
like ixora clusters and hairy figs pink
dusk ceiling fans twirling slow tongues
savouring de-skinned spice mangoes—
golden flesh in descending night
kulfi for dessert—an Indian ice cream
almonds sparkling in eyes mourning
doves moaning in grass, above oak
limbs rubbing gutters and brown shingles

* An Indian fruit (Syzygium cumini) also known as Indian blackberry; intro-
duced to Guyana, the West Indies and other areas by Indian indentured labour-
ers. Now widely grown in the Americas, Asia, and other areas.

3

And you will walk the dog
as always a brown canine
cat-sized led and leading
down strange alleys and off-pave
and you will yearn for someone
else by your side another presence
another pup leashed and leashing
dusk into evening into newsprint
room—books on walls books
on shelves among dawn bamboos
misted and howler monkeys calling
at B Line*—designed by Dutch canal artists

* A canal separating the districts of Canal No 1 Polder from Canal No 2 Polder

Excite

Not cereal in milk-bowl
organic and brown as your skin—
jettisoning instructions creating
good money down the drain

Not swishing rain or leaves
dancing shadows in full sun
through ceiling to floor glass

Nothing rousing us anymore
not name in book or review
not romance—f—k instructors
on negatives and prepositions
clinging to artifice like pigs
to garbage foraging for diamonds

Not summer thighs defying tides
rising waters O heat O heat O heat

Stalking Birds

Grackles searching morning grass
swaying outside the Central Bank
black busts of non-aligned leaders
black birds clucking like hens
announcing just delivered eggs
generational hope until you crack
shells over frying pans—fertilized
or unfertilized a tightrope science
in prolife minds tissue cells incubating
crows cawing outside in November
dry wetlands indistinguishable
in this flushed dawn starlings swarming
hawk stalking flash-of-fire-feathers—
cardinal you say seducing boys
from pulpits disturbed by snowy
gaulings* flapping—leave me leave
your seeking congruence for home

---

*   Egret

Thanksgiving

Sun dances through clear-glass door
flagged by palm fronds waving
webbed arms to bladed banana
leaf-shadow lounging on fence
a morning thief dropping red petals
on clipped lawn Indian orchid hearts
rolling wind circumambulating
my south your south warm jamun
leaves dancing on weathered fence

Patio Table

From this distance through caked glass
from this door sliding two ways
surface like winter cypress waving
in wind two chairs one cluttered—
shears a summer hat marigold seeds—
another empty utterance now prophecy
a college town's clutch of books
curved letters on paper pink fingers
on black keyboard decorated with bling
one thousand count cotton sheets
milk and toast in dawns ringed by
bamboos and bearded oaks again
lest morning stubble bruise your chin

Only through this speckled door
chairs, a table's weathered top vacated

Four Miles in Flatwoods Park

By the time we arrive at the trailhead
the warm vehicle, the drive home, garage
door retracting overhead, we will forget

This cyclist sailing past, thin ankles, heavy
midsection—Armstrong before Armstrong
we will forget this flow on the berm
left foot, right foot, breathe in breathe out

We will forget job cuts, the new database
a hawk gliding to a limb without flapping
chirping wrens bobbing up from grass
freshcut in summerlike winter afternoon

The machine's metal tracks a tank's
imprinted in the damp slope the cleared bottom
at the foot of trees mulched stumps, hundred
feet oaks and pines sawdust—*remember Katrina*
every beauty every named demonized in a storm
the levees around New Orleans breached
because roots penetrated dams—flood water
widening cracks into floodgates will not occur here

We forget this asphalt trail straddles a dyke
screeching squirrels catbirds calling in brush
like kittens, the wren's double tweet round
as a dholak's overtaken by motorized skateboard

Cheater cheater legs on fire at mile one
descending dam, tar-trail damp over creek
swirling broken limbs from last night's storm
a runner intent on records, the flatwoods grass

Finally brown from last week's freeze like
reaped wheat fields, wasted paddies—we will walk
four miles today in weak sunshine
autumn comes midwinter to Florida oaks
brass-yellow and still as our Shiva murti

On the plantshelf gathering dust, we will forget
dog poop on blacktop, dog poop in grass
scented owners thinking f—k the Poop & Scoop
sign—dogophile dogophobe approaching mile two
marker swamps to left and right another snake

Sliding over the bitumen pausing to watch
the recoil in your eyes—you, named for serpent
lord, serpent god, snakeophile, snakeophobe
if you say one word, one phrase incorrect
turning back past denuded trees silver-marble

Like the Taj with Shiva's trishul—trident—on top
a twig like a Hindu kalash, a denuded coconut
on five mango leaves on a lota atop the Mahal's
finial—crowning glory of Mughalai theft—
mother of mother India—father of my fathers

Forgetting until a blue-shoed runner passes
on the left, legs like tiger's, buttocks cupping
shorts in upstroke downstroke ponytail flapping
we will forget by the time we arrive at the car
we are young young young again donning

Athletic pants white-striped down legs—
what we did not come to see what we did not
come to feel or remember desire a memory
risen like wildfire from smoldering wildlife

receding in the runner's rear straggler white
wildflowers yellow wildflowers in this
summer-autumn–winter-summer Florida
winter—imaging Shakespeare in writing school

Pleasures of Green

The trees have dressed. Latespring Florida
a northern summer—keep your whites
and browns and blacks in that cloud cover
bearing water for elsewhere, thin as a strainer
for southern sun above road rising above steel
belted radials starlings cry grackles call redstart
a wren—mockingbirds deplaning on lawn

What brings you here to my slice of pie—
worms, grubs I cannot see in the carwaxed
day awaiting a shine and buffer's cloth
we do not cry for left-behind—this is home
keep your whites and blacks and browns—
give me green give me green give me green

Waiting for Yamraj

for Raj (Radharaman Upadhyaya 1957-2016)

This wasn't who we were. A faltered voice
above bedside commode. Visiting holy sites
in that holy land reconnecting: We change
ourselves not the world. Here's a banana.
Would you like some Prasad—you shared ·
sacred fruits, food of the Gods consecrated,
offered sacrifices to flames in khunds*
for others—hundreds, thousands: may
you live long. May your offspring prosper.
May you live for a 1,000 years—for others:
Oblations to you Shiva. Oblations to you Kali
Rama, Vishnu, Durga. Oblations Nataraja
may your fire spread through the three worlds
may you consume this caner, may these ashes
fertilize our earth. All we've learned unlearn

This isn't who we were, are: waiting for Yama**

---

* A small metal vessel in which a sacrificial flame is lit during a puja, or prayer
ceremony. In ancient times, a small geometric hole in the ground served this
purpose.
** Or Yamraj—the lord, or God of death

Waiting for the Black Car

When the black car comes to your door
you are gone already. Not black British
taxis, not limousines. You are a body.
Home hospice—no facility for the aged
un-tended by jaded attendants—in full
sun. Not this half-lit dawn when dew drips
like lovers tongues and lips in a parting
kiss—be gone. If only we could recapture—
you remember. I don't. A gender thing
women have longer memories an excuse
—early Alzheimer's, muscles atrophying
dew falling from eves. Cutting grass
this morning when night moisture dries
in summer heat when the black car comes
you are already a lesser body than your body

May Sunsets

These croaking frogs know something in spring
dusk undressing like a slow striptease
turmeric in a bowl with a pinch of salt—
correcting your Hindi-Sanskrit pronunciation
red wing, ginger head, ginger ale, ground
thickening split-peas soup, the neighbourhood asses
braying and bucking on the Cummins Canal dam
after a decade two bats becoming four—
the flies the flies and zika-bearing mosquitoes
disrupting Olympics and the Brazilian bottoms
in the smallest threads in the largest carnival
jeera, haldi, carrot flecks, channa-dal—all kala mircha
in a dusk now aged like wine from a forgotten brew

Funeral and Cremation

It was how we journeyed up the Garden State
Parkway that first time in an autumn night
no GPS no cell phone—AAA maps left behind
directions on land lines written in your journal
clear and sloped like grass in the NE Trade Wind

And when the turns were wrong—north given
as south—payphone still working, we found
a quarter near that bikers' tavern, metals clinking
shimmering spikes and crosses: "wrong directions

Brother? I was born in this town." "Wrong recorder"
you laughed trusting the world blaming none.
Will that biker vote for Trump, today Brexit—
we must control our borders, the invading hordes.
Biological brother threading sister would not come
down at first we rung the doorbell tentatively

Calling again from a rotary phone across the street.
We are tired brother, returning from a long flight
to South America, he said—seeing you off
today they descend—brothersisterhusbandwife
—as they wheel you into a chapel you visited

A hundred times as pandit performing last rites

Coffin rolled into crematorium, the needle rising
with heat, an official opening a small portal
for family—see, there is no fire fraud here
red flames leaping out like tongues in laughter
the way we journeyed down the Garden State
Parkway laughing at misdirection: *Good thing you*
were with me: nobody would have believed. Nobody.

El Nino July

1

Where has June gone in July's rain
wet grass sticking to the mower's wheels
black ants along fence a squirrel sprints
across the patio's abeer bricks sunburnt
faces discolored by July's slaps red-singed
borders coleus cheeks a childhood vintage
white periwinkles hugging a pot's bottom
two lizards cohabiting on a middle runner
in the open leaves rustling the jay's screams
are all bees honey bees?—a duck's flight
arrow in our hearts lavender crape myrtle
edging the wetlands in a blueless July

2

July ticking in dripping dew off eves
on concrete on shrubbery on gravel
river stones and pebbles transported
from Home Depot in a hundred years
will the store still stand will beetles
still chirp outside our predawn door
dreading sunrise—to live you must
make a living shave shower encase limbs
in business casuals in the subtropical
South taking to highways to cubicles
digital serfs—but July still drips away
as it always has for a thousand years
cicadas humming what do you do when
rains intensify when water laps our door

Scent of Florida

Working the lawn mower back and forth
diagonally we smell of this state—
swamp-rank stuck to sweatwet cotton jersey
evening shadows lengthening in August
the buzz is neither Rio's Olympics nor
Trump's comments retweeted

A blue bird calls from the swamp campaigning
for presidents, the buzzing is of no consequence
we do not plan to father more children—still
beware zika and lightening and the first drops
preceding thunder and the earth vibrating
as we race for shelter laughing—nothing
quite compares to the scent of Florida

In This Shrubbery

Darjeeling this morning. A thin mist rising
from the steaming cup. There are no hillsides
on this Florida flatland. Heart-leafed shammi
bends to the wild lawn. It is not the golden
marigold dancing in dawn sun that wakes
this day, or the scent of tea from Assam—
the foolery of a cardinal more flaming
than fire in the shrubbery chasing a female
exulting like steelpans then silence. Sex sex sex

Commotion

Next to the bagged Sunday newspaper
on the driveway, a buzzing caught our ears.
It wasn't cicadas rattling the early morning
news of the world or the girl at the phone
kiosk explaining *I am Kurdish, you say*
my name "Ala" not "Allah" like Arabic god.
We will never pass through the Countryside
Mall again, a Moroccan male's companion
Kurdish woman's voice still in our heads

The honey bee losing a wing struggling
to right itself in the robellini palm's shade
to fend off the swam and we could hear it
say: I am not dead yet and we could not bear
the red ants swarming as we set her free
knowing that bees do not regenerate wings

Crematorium in NYC

Here in brilliant June sun, jets taking off
from La Guardia, we sprinkle no dry flour
by the door for tomorrow's imprint—
feet of bird, paw of beast, a fish's fin,
or nothing, will tell where goes your soul

Ancient custom—here among grandfather oaks
and swaying elms, the throb of a city
that fails to sleep, the expressway humming
faint among white and black and white
apparel and the babble of old acquaintances

Here where you performed last rites
more times than anyone will ever know
we do today for you waiting for the press
of a button and the roaring furnace, right
heat—which ash is yours, which ash ours

Thunderstorms, Toronto

In this autumn storm we stare
at the water's grey wall obliterating
waves on the lake roaring on honey
sand not touching toes. In this autumn
storm we stop at amber lights and red
skidding slightly on tramcar tracks
turning away from The Beaches
maples raging in wind we take stairs
finger on lips quietly keying
lock and kicking off footwear

At the door a flute following us
into a tiny kitchen—are these oak
polished with usage—Indian tea
but whose toes we touch Devi
dancing in the Krishna temple
abandon in fingers unhitching belt
zipper pen—white panties to floor
a story we can't remember from Latvia
or Lithuania or Ukraine another Indra
taking us to Goberdhan Mountain
Krishna improvising umbrella
from stone in this autumn rain
thunderstorm nipples touching white
cotton in an ancient puja
and your one-legged dance, Shiva

Puerto Rican Espousing Julia de Burgos*

On fine mesh, leaves spill Atlantic drizzle
in dark shadows riding a tea-weak sun
we know how waves rattle seawall
how tides rip greenheart pilings
beneath our soles through large creases
wafting in these branches we clutch
keys falling through cracks
lost lost lost except for spring toes
in October's green skirt swirling
in wind we are as carefree as we will
never know again in drunken swaying
limbs on chlorophyll deck and fine mesh
a solar screen—why does your sea run in me

---

*   Puerto Rican poet

25

Exiles Retreating South

Raised arm bathed in sunshine—
how else can we see swimmer
between cheek and chin—eyes
of Roman conqueror or god. How
far to Naples to Venice. Geographies
over bare shoulders. Is this it, then
all those monuments we couldn't
complete, the legions one mile short
of northern bastions—the mountains

Aye, the mountains unconquerable,
retreating to Hadrian's Wall to stay
barbarians—painted faces foreheads
vertical lines horizontal lines
like that on lingams in sacred corners
your sea retreating further south
across the water—a mile short

Horsemen and infantry looking back
next time—there will be no next time
a flute calls citrus blossoms Mediterranean
scents on breasts we cannot wait to see
O native land O native land before
tectonic shifts we were, once, one earth

Diwali: Sailing From India

We fled west "following the Light
of the sun." No land in sight
flapping sails a monotonous song.
Board on deck—if we could find
some curry leaves, any leaves
in troughs, waves as tall as masks
—canvas or cotton—a bird, two
branches in the tide at sunset
turmeric clouds turmeric leaves
glowing and fencing light—you turn
away hustling to your berth—
no word for such swaying
hips in cypresses on a far shoreline
tomorrow, elsewhere in the dawn
sand and sun and land O land O land
tonight we light one diya—earthern
vessel, barge, boat, laden with oil
an unextinguished flame whispering
a prayer to Lakshmi

Kalinyas and Manaharva at Jonestown[*]

On a hill overlooking Kaituma, eagles
searched, one dropping like a fighter-jet

bushmaster snake no match for harpy
and Kalinyas the Carib kaseek said

Yankees when they travel want to carry
their their whole country on their backs

Manaharva. Returning from Nebraska
Manaharva finally believed the old man

Lapsing into silence paddling the Barima
River zigging like a snake and arriving

Via a shortcut. Buildings vandalized
rotting, the Carib jungle retaking cottages

Nobody asked our permission, not Americans
not government officials not the Spanish

Or Dutch before them, or the English all gone
joining our ancestors. They clapped and sang

---

[*] A reference to the most moving essay on Jonestown (Guyana) by, now, deceased novelist, poet, and historian (and professor at the University of Nebraska), Jan Carew, on a visit to the site after the murder-suicide precipitated by cult leader, Jim Jones. Carew was accompanied on the trip by his great-uncle, a Kaseek (a Carib chief) from the area, and who was nearby during the tragedy, which resulted in the deaths of almost 900 Americans in the Jonestown commune in the Guyana bush, part of the Amazon region. As a boy, Carew spent may vacations with his Carib relatives in the area—Manaharva was his Carib name.

And dropped one by one. A thousand
foreigners dead by nightfall—I walked

Among them with candleflies-in-bottle lamps
lighting my way chanting the Carib deathsongs

And more yankees and strangers came writing
books and novels and poems on Jonestown

Really about themselves—where are they now?
nothing about Kaituma, land of the everlasting

Dreamers, heartland of the Caribs, nothing of us
nothing about our people, Manaharva

You have written deeply and soaring
as the harpy—our souls among these stars

Manaharva, our souls walking in these stars

Welcoming the New Year without "Uncle Ram"

For Milton Ramgobin 1927-2017

We stand with a tree in hand
several across the roaring street
silvered pussy willow naked
in January another year—whose calendar
—your body finally becoming shell
your consciousness gone, its unique voice
inimitable inflections from your long
London sojourn before fleeing rain wet cold
thick fogs bracketing days and nights
yet—*Wha wrang widh you bhai*—
A lilt of the ancient county, Berbice
some say, you and I knowing timbre
going beyond to UP and Tamil Nadu
grands and great-grands and great great
grands following the old railway
tracks to New Amsterdam—*what
is this life* you quipped breaking silence
soaking in night drizzling on Georgetown
facing southern stars peeping into souls

As now when all remaining are ashes
we wait to cool, gather from the gas
crematorium—*You know the Madrassi
—some of them sing and dance at death
and cry at birth* you laughed we all
laugh this January when neem and pear
are still green—British pear in colonial
childhoods in British Guiana your other
quip at avocado the deepest chlorophyll

hue we've seen in this Florida winter
sun sparkling bronze and India-lota brass
dogs barking and wagging tails
the Indian orchid tree blooming—
a red Jhandi-flag gyrating in the wind

Through Mists

In this early morning some call night
we suddenly enter cloud fog
where is your bonnet your two headlights
lost in a whiteness pliable like dough
or moist knuckles kneading prairie flour

Skin like sada roti fresh from a fireside
in this morning some call night commuting
to heaven and pataal—cotton-candy dense
we barely see hood—combustible panic
in our chests would explode on arteries
we travel every day suddenly strange
the window glass cold this silence louder
than jungle—we will get through this patch
if we keep motoring on—and we do

When sunrise comes will we laugh
and look back and out from our desks
at full sun—a sliver moon enveloped
in this dense whiteness some call night—when
will I see you again when will I see you again

For Alvin*

Some people want to sleep
when Lillie and Thompson
tek new ball. Not me. Not Kalli
crouching over bat like tiger cat—
jaguar self. You could hear klack
klack klack leather ball flying over boundary
from down under. Kalli one end

And Freddie.** Transistor clear as whistle
in a cool night under neighbour Thinney
five-finger tree. Centuries in England
again in first World Cup at Lords's, lord
every time Lillie bounce is hook and boundary
and when Packer bribe Lloyd and company
is who lead young West Indies—
if you think is submarine
think again, is not even batting machine

Multi-charmed God, willow tongue lolling
on sparkling Bourda Green***—
is Kalli is Kalli is Kalli-Charran

* Alvin Kallicharran former captain of the West Indies cricket team, a brilliant and gifted cricketer and one of the great batsman of the sport, who (it was widely held by cricket fans) was treated very badly by the West Indies Cricket Board and West Indies cricket, and unfairly discarded (along with others) as captain, once the other top team players—who had deserted and dumped the official West Indies team (as many players from other nations did their national team) to play in the rebel Kerry Packer series (1977-1979, organized by Australian media tycoon, Kerry Packer) in Australia for more money—returned.
** Roy Fredericks, a fine and gifted opening batsman for Guyana and the West Indies.
*** Once, one of the finest cricket fields in the world and the venue for Test matches against touring national team played in Guyana; over the last decade, no longer used for cricket's primary version of the game (Test matches)—since a new stadium and cricket field was built.

Samans* on Main Street

We glide north under red star bursts to ocean
strolling in the Avenue between
Main Street's one-way lanes—not south
to the city's innards or the Amazon's belly

We glide north among red star bursts
canopying our stroll to the Atlantic
dappled sunshine like blinking fairy lights
on faces leaving the Cenotaph behind

And the Tower Hotel we entered once
only through service rear doors—our skins
not white enough our eyes too brown
to see sun-bronzed tree-trimmers

Like sakie-winkie monkeys high high
on thick tree limbs—saman from Asia
throwing red stars in the upper canopy on parapets
when Jagan** strode through The Tower's front door

Declaring from now Amerindians blacks Indians . . .
will enter from the front if they choose—
we glide pass colonial transplants flaming overhead
on our way to the Atlantic on our way to the North

---

*   The royal poinciana tree introduced to Guyana and the West Indies from Asia.
**   Dr. Chedi Jagan, first elected Chief Minister (1953) and, later, first elected
Premier (1961) of British Guiana; after independence from the British in 1966
and a series of rigged elections by a brutal, de factor, dictatorship that kept him
out of office, he became the first democratically elected President of Guyana
(1992) under internationally monitored elections. He died in office in 1997.

Waterloo: At Siewdass Sadhu's Temple in the Sea*

When you passed, pausing like a helicopter
we stood on a mountain lookout chattering
like parrots—a most wondrous sight at night
Port-of-Spain crawling up down valley sides

Somewhere hidden in lights, Laventille
we skirt like an audience staring at curtains
in a St Lucian's theatre. Do not go there
warn our hosts. Ah, you haven't seen

The lights from Shimla, my friend—but
Nothing, nothing—floury phulowrie**
like weak tea, no daal in the mixture
mouths professor UP to professor Delhi:
kya kya karilla***—haha—you mean Karille.

---

* Denied permission to build a Hindu temple on sugar estate land in 1947 in
colonial Trinidad, and jailed for the temple he constructed (which was demol-
ished), Siewdass built a small island offshore (and a causeway to it) almost single-
handed over 25 years, often carting buckets of soil on his cycle handle-bars. He
erected a temple on the island he constructed. The site/island, which now has a
new temple, is a National Treasure of Trinidad and Tobago.
** A small spherical snack made from a dough mixture of ground split-peas
and flour and deep fried. Served with chatney or achaar, originally at Indo-Ca-
ribbean functions in Guyana, Jamaica, Trinidad and Suriname, now a popular
food across all ethnic groups in these countries and in the Indo-Caribbean
and Caribbean diaspora. Many commercial establishments and vendors make
and sell a watered down version, with more flour and little or no ground split
peas in the mixture.
*** Bitter gourd (karille in Trinidad); in Guyana, everyone across all ethnic
groups knew and called bitter gourd by this Indian name

35

I am Indian, too, you know, my father Shyam
Khalil—the vendor's dougla* infants fading
into dusk behind another stall and trays laden
with mangoes and bananas from Couva.

We do not want to go just yet into St James
into Nepaul Street into Movietown to see
our ethnicity on screen off screen—it is safe
to ride south under that overpass bypassing
Caroni Swamp, or a drizzle in Chaguanas

On the way pausing at Lion House boarded up
a whorehouse next door. What mongooses
procured in London afternoons seeking that
at home we couldn't desire: temple decorated
by mist and mountains hemming the capital.

I turn away, Hanuman,** from sea-stench-silt
like liquid ash on sand at low tide, discarded
diyas brown like your face, saffron like winter
breasts uncovered from flurries, a wan sun

* The Hindi word for someone of mixed race, used in Guyana, Jamaica, Trinidad and Suriname primarily to refer to someone of mixed Indian and African ancestries.
** One of the many forms of God in Hinduism. Hanuman puja (prayer-ceremony) is very popular in the Guyana, Jamaica, Trinidad and Suriname and in India; and the Hanuman Chalisa (a poem in forty verses) is sung at these pujas. A shape-shifter, Hanuman is popularly depicted with the face of a monkey (and a tail), on a human body—derogatorily referred to by Christian missionaries to India as the "monkey God." Hanuman is a symbol of strength, loyalty, courage and persistence. In *A House for Mr. Biswas*, Naipaul called his maternal family home in Trinidad, "Hanuman House."

An apple, or two anemic red globs streaked
by white cultivated in northern orchards—
no mangoes, no bananas sourced from this land
no coconut fluting thrushes in the Trades
instead two honey-roast dogs roaming the path.

The temple locked! We search for bricks
laid by Siewdass in this sea, dirt bucketed in
on bicycle handlebars, where are taans* singing
your daily treks: one-one-dutty building dam
—no might of China yet greater on your island
in the sea, this Mandir in an ocean you crossed
giving a Wiki tale to Wiki news, fake history

Fake Brahmins, flake descendants crying aye
aye aye—baap-re-baap! You lose caste
crossing water neither black nor time nor his-
tory, pain these women singing in skits
pain these children dramatizing on stage, pain

In ajie'e** head: we are singing birahas and
dancing like tops gyrating on a polished table
only there is no end to talk and conferences
no end to parrot chatter, roosters crowing
hens challenging cocks: we do not need
overheavy combs, thick spurs, fancy feathers

---

*   A fast, rhythmic form of Indian classical music sung in Guyana, Jamaica,
Trinidad and Suriname, and the origin/source of the "chatney/chutney"
music of these countries and of the Caribbean.
**   Paternal grandmother. Indian/Hindi word.

37

Or sixty seconds squiggles. I will not have
you on my back—a hen a hen another
who will fuck me to my face, who will hold
me all night, who will devour dildoed
cunt, who will let me come when I want, go

When I'm sated, creole this language I
free to tongue not daru* bottle drained
and dead, not rice belly flapping behind
in front like coconut jelly nah grow up.

We walk from Tunapuna to St. Augustine
dorms, to Jamaica House all night temple girls
to Trini House for morning tea nice nice
arriving at this temple in the sea—Sadhu limbs
tough like steel, Sadhu waist flat like thawa**—
no roti belly, no cockass squiggly thing—

Pathway straight like arrow, scrotum bag
ejaculating sea, evacuating Gulf of Paria water.
No shirt of pauper, no pants of submission
no beggar of Bay, no curry favouring
yes, massa. Yes, massa with pranaam palms
yes, sahib. Yes sahib. Yes, sardar. Quickie
between cane rows—how cane bitter you say

Nahi*** nahi nahi! Cane sweet, sweet
O sadhu, sweet like sweat, smooth
like finger trampling causeway to sky—
who owns this ocean, this graveyard to God?

---

*   Rum, liquor. Indian/Hindi word.
**   A flat baking iron on which roti is cooked. Indian/Hindi word.
***   No. From Hindi.

No pain like this body a chant to sheep
no pleasure like this body a dhun* to I
and I and I advaita,** I this dvaita***
clouds trying to conceal the northern range
ringing Port-of-Spain haze over valley

Kiskadee rivalling the afternoon schoolbell
ringing out class, Hanuman, defying rain
eight-five feet high. Not north India or south
not Ceylon or Sri Lanka taller, man, I tell you
not ficus ficus to one side, not peepal another
even here a spear-heart point and palms

Swaying mangoes fattening on trees, ixoras
like pepper guarding fences, when you pass
you pass except this temple in samudra
until the ice caps melt, until oceans rise
I shall remain, I shall remain like those
mountains to the north ringing Port-of-Spain.

* A light composition based on Indian ragas; in the Caribbean, more com-
monly sung at religious functions.
** The Indian philosophy/school of non-dualism.
*** The Indian philosophy/school of dualism.

Badhase Maharaj*

White frock white orhni unconcealing shaven
head sometimes a stubble like mowed grey grass
laughing at everything above roaring wind
outside teasing tall coconuts and laden guineps
rocking in our hammock asking nothing, not roti
and curried dinner we offered, just vanishing
for months like monarch butterflies to Trinidad

Returning slower—"Auntie Badhase coming!"
someone shouting—a parrot chattering
with everyone down Owen Street, daddy allowing
a sip of XM**—an exception for this pastel woman

Who shaved her head who wore white only,
except olive rubber slippers straps, whose
sobriquet was Badhase Maraj, or simply Badhase!
"Pagal!" someone whispering behind her back
"When he left her, she went crazy!" Not to us

Not to children. Rocking in our hallway, softly
chanting in Hindi, dreaming in our hammock of a flat
in Curepe, a warehouse in Laventille, a mansion in Valsayn
or Tunapuna, kiskadees floating down the Northern Range
mist and rain—I bring you laughter and a parrot's chatter
—My name is Badhase Maraj and I going "Chinidad!"

* The nickname for a woman from Guyana, who reportedly knew Badhase
Maraj, the Trinidadian politician and Hindu rights activist. A rags to riches
story, he made his first million dollars by the time he was 30, acquiring surplus
supplies when the Americans closed their base after the end of the second
world war. He was the first and, perhaps, the most powerful leader of Indians
in the twin-island nation, building several Hindu schools in the country at a
time when the Indian literacy rate was 50%—and gave Indians a sense of pride
in themselves. He was only 52 when he died in 1971.
** A rum manufactured in Guyana

Evening Song

In a jamun evening when gaulings clip
my hair and you ask what is gauling—
in this sindoor sky when egrets light
our temples and you ask what is sindoor

In a jamun evening while bats dance
before vermilion clouds and we glance
askance at alien eyes—spring garden
rumpled with weeds, dried vines
overgrowing cheeks—questions on lips

In a jamun dusk when cattle birds glow
like silver on my head and you whisper
come to Pompey or tap out texts
of Kolkata and Shimla—Atlantic surf
crashing on chests like coconut milk

In a jamun light slipping into sea
curiosity sated for now in our refrain
—where are those fingers would lip
temples we entered for Kali's tongue
thick with mantras and mystic chants
arresting Yama for one more night

This Shore

Let us stand under sea-willow
as sun and water rise—tide taking
land and houses raised too close
to shore for waves scrubbing sand
for a roll of dolphins feeding
for a triumphant cry of gulls
for crests quarreling and crashing
on themselves, let us hover under willow
as this golden yolk melts into ocean
as ebb takes ash—repurposed
skin and bone and maya's trophies
to another shore—as twilight spreads
and candles twitter lightyears overhead
let us dance tandavs igniting this shore

Shadows on our skins

If you think silk was only white
you didn't see night-skinned nani—
great grandma really, a twigbreeze swaying
in a honeybrown hammock—jute
bag unlayered from Demerara crystals

If you think silk was only white
you didn't see me, jahajin*, in Chaguanas
India ink from toe to hair tips

Strands illuminating Oxford blankets
O night O night O night
I am she I am he I am she
Shivoham Shivoham Shivoham

---

* Jahajin – Female shipmate; on the three-month sea voyage from India,
Indian indentured labourers developed life-long bonds

In America

Here we don't take to streets for ourselves
or overturn cars or set stores aflame

We give you halves: Gita or Gandhi
one manual on yoga, the other ahimsa

Here you tell us yoga has nothing
to do with Hinduism—a billion dollar
outfitting of throbbing pudendums
muscled rears, a Lopez singing

Here we give you Patels and Persauds
chant Silicon Valley dhuns of doctors
motel-keepers and smug *CEOs-Indica*

Here we flip properties instead of cars
turned on burning roofs project gay faces
scribble poesy you see left and left and left

Bush Fires

Blue muslin veils fence and wetland
pines. Evil is afoot. Why sirens exult
like jays, why proud sun is contained
in chiffon deflecting bloodlight on leaves
and birds sailing into woods. Byzantium
Byzantium. Authur's pyre drifting in haze
fire replaying an ancient rage.
We smell ash ducking back inside—
Flatwoods burns. Starkey Preserve burns
—two hundred acres. Seven hundred. I-
75 closed. Thin smoke a magic curtain
outside—we are far too far from the burn

Repurposing the Library

I turn in this archipelago and the crystal
sands of Demerara like fallen greenheart
leaves are crackling—there is a drought
in Florida. Fire sears cabbage palms
and underbrush, the prickly grass black
to the highway shoulder. A stray cigarette
butt from a pickup truck—it was no spark
of lightening no exhaust misfire no
instantaneous combustion—the library selling
books to unburden itself of itself. Take out
shelves—more space for computers
A dancing floor—I turn on this peninsula
like a worm on itself—book nazi, dharma bum
the essential Raleigh searching again in Guiana
for a lie: El Dorado—tutoring at tables
teachers moonshining—not for all the gold
sunlight flashing on pond—the books have left
the library. Not I not I turning for the door

Before and After Temple

We can scent body with sandalwood
cleanse skin with haldi* arriving—
enthralling ragas transported in dholaks
the harmonium's notes chording
with voice—no longer German
forgetting purpose—to chastise India

We can adorn bodies in Benaras saris flowing
kurtas forgetting whose fingers plucked cotton
it isn't all mechanized on factory looms
Mohandas greeting Lancashire mill workers
in homespun—good evening good morning
goodbye—you've displaced our spinners
and what is this wheel of change—let me sing
a hymn O King George O King George
Georgie—after me—King George King George

We can spend all night celebrating jayanties
of Hanuman or Sita or ratris—glorious dancing
but the last bell reverberates aarti's flames
scent of camphor petals at Kali's feet perfuming
altar palms kissing palms wick igniting ghi
and Sattie Lila Chandra swaying
O God O God O god is this why we came

---

*   Turmeric

For prasad—fig bananas pomegranates pera[*]
sugar-browned Mohanbhog[**] ghi-crisp roth[***]
foods from God your offering—but the last chant
is finished. We take the flames benediction—
night laden with stars one glimpse
through spectacles before we depart
fingers touching beneath paper bag—Prasadam

Untranslatable. Tomorrow in the bold morning
light when cocks crow when militias
shoulder arms on Sheriff Street when we whip
out Kali and Krishna no longer sensuous
tongue or loverboy—Kali of the thousand
arms Krishna of a thousand chakras
waving a thousand Gitas—this is no time
for philosophy no time for Radha-yoginis

Breathing bending curving practicing trading
Sex sex sex and sex doing what must be
done—even Gandhi knew the king of yogas
was karma—tandav in Shiva's toes
Pakawaj fingers igniting taut skin

---

[*]   Also known as peda; a small, sweet, round snack of Indian origin prepared
with milk, sugar, and spices
[**]   Mohanbhog (on Mohan Bhog), literally Mohan's food (i.e. the food of
God, Krishna—Mohan is another name for Krishnna); a sweet dish/food
made mainly with milk, flour, sugar, ghi and spices; made mainly during Indian
festivals and consecrated and served during or after pujas/religious functions in
Guyana and the West Indies
[***]   A crisp, sweet, round, Indian snack, somewhat like a roti, fried in ghi; in
Guyana and the West Indies; prepared mainly during Indian festivals and at
pujas/prayer ceremonies

Morning Invocations

Just before the century turned
we were to redeem promises
we could not keep—all predictions
were wrong—there is no sunshine

Morning palms are still and silent
with guilt the orchids veering off side
did we see anything at that cricket
match—Bourda you said a Dutch word

Swamp cypresses pierce sky
like jagged spearheads dusted off
at an ancient site by archeologists
—these are things you'll want to see

Things I cannot give—this time
I make no promises I cannot keep

From the Beaches, Toronto

Sand lining blue sandals—snakeskin
or imitation alligator. These are all
we think in Florida. Watch any water.
Watch lightening on wave. A post fried
last summer. Thunderclap. Blue ocean
turning green with land's phlegm:
weeds, lawn clippings, fertilizer, plastic.

It isn't even a flowered notebook words
on space-blue and grey-black gravel
pieces of asphalt, the metal bottle you lip.

Who said: let us go to Woodbine before—
rain coming down on Queen Street
streetcar tracks slippery. I troll further east
on the Rogue Beach, Scarborough Bluffs
showing layers on layers of sediment.

How high had the oceans risen, our screams
punctuating pillows in your one-limbed
dance, Shiva, from a Baltic seashore cabin.
In the beginning, orchid toes. The left flaking,
ringed sand touched and touching fingers
and face—how once we worshipped
leaving & taking the Beaches to bedroom

Toronto Unnamed

In this one hundred fiftieth, or thousandth,
year of our love, we still make promises
we can't keep, dew dripping down
eves, Usha—the dawn—and we still
can't utter your name lest the CN Tower
break lest the Ontario Science Centre crack
and roll unto that hillock—how do you make
love in public dipping into the Don valley!—
lest our hearts burst again touching footwear
discarded on grass kissing toes decorated
with fragments from land from lake from sea.

But sandals still sit on your throne,
O Rama*, until we return from banwaas** to cherry
blooms inundating the Escarpment, a surf
of sparrows' songs cleansing morning rain rattling
zinc roofs, roosters crowing sleep from ears from eyes
on showy ash, maple keys, crabapples and paper
birch limbs—look out, you call, dried coconuts fall
in high wind like promises: I will return, I will return

to sit at your feet, to sip of love, to chant your name

---

* In the Ramayana, when Rama was sent into exile for 14 years, his brother
placed a pair of his (Rama's) sandals on the throne to symbolize that he was
ruling on behalf of Rama, until Rama's returned from exile
** Exile; also forest

Snow Came Early

Winter came early in November—storm whiting
everything. It wasn't only cold insulated
the automobile heater fan blowing furiously
snow raging outside, night closing faster
than we hoped—no choice but to cancel dinner
no time to dwell on past missteps, snow cakes
drifting in layers on the Bloor Bridge headlights
curving in the Valley below where we head
away from glass towers multiplying like
mosquitoes since our last visit more flakes
bindis on windshield third eyes fourth fifth—

Just vehicle and I in forever commutes memoried
radio repeating over and again the obvious—
snow came earlier than expected earlier
than forecast on a ramp your remember as if last
night—avoid this icy downcurving shoulder
into the Don Valley merging into Ant-line lights
snow lifting from tyre grooves like mud
on the old loam road in Canal No 2 Polder
devised by the departed Dutch—here English
on the road to Scarborough and everywhere
we are still alone in the ravine's white night

Remembering 1966, After Solzhenitsyn

Travelling on an updraft or downdraft
on Easter Day 1966 or weeks later
currents from Russia or South America
we breathed the same air Alexander—

Mommy passing—How painters paint
using wild brush strokes to convey essence
waiting fifty years after the revolution
for an orthodox religious procession

Repeating traditions of forebears
while socialist youths thug along—
she drank straight from the bottle
after putting on bathing suit after

Posing for a picture. If I could
ask you father: why why why
fifty years later, did you weep
for eyes for breasts for lips for legs

What we did or didn't a haunting
beyond impressionist paintings "Scream"
"Howl" we don't blur canvas Solzhenitsyn
realism a face like Arctic mask and mouths

that will not weep. Usage is sun
on a ship engulfed by sea. What
means Picasso's lines and why is
Van Gogh clearer you don't care

Except, what price for that canvas

Would break Siberian winds bearing
down on Moscow or tropical rain storms
in the Guyana bush as you recorded
Easter 1966 or after—and fifty years later

And one, we pen missives for the same
generals and marxist-leninist proletariats

In militia procession dancing on memory
and history—ritual of religion of sex
of work of commute of carnival still ritual

Overcast

Households sleep and dawn is still
quiet. Even birds take morning
breaks. We are waiting for light—
to transpond a photon not even
to outer space or to moons. New York
would do or Paris' poop-stained streets
and hijab-inflected cafes here defiance
sex oozing out tight jeans seams
your head covered with cloth grown
beyond sunrises. What happened
to your painted toes exposed to dust
to dirt to leering men in America
—bikini and sex and coca-cola country
you can even burn the flag or drape
it over morning's head like asphalt
clouds—but that star will still out
to our calls—give me sun give me sun

Removing Monuments

Smoke emanating from agarbati merging
in sightline with hot air balloons
rising from the Pride Field like azaleas
in Augusta blooming before the Masters

Golf clubs kicking up sacred turf
propelling white balls into water into holes
soil red from above in a flying apparatus

Easily mistaken for blood-soaked cloths of
civil war amputees—Europeans and Africans
asking: where are you from? Natives eroded
in a white night in the Guyana bush

900 dead and Kalinyas the Carib Kaseek
lamenting—they did not ask permission
to take our ancestral lands—I walked among
their dead unnoticed holding a candle-fly

Lamp and then planes came and the military
with body bags—General Lee you must come
down from your stone horse General Lee
you must evacuate the courthouse square

Or was that Keats across the pond—do not go
quiet into the night—rage rage rage holding
aloft a German flag or green bands in India
will we chant for the minarets erected on razed
temple stones to come down for flake Arabic
inscriptions in the Taj's temple to be removed
to graveyards in Arabia or Turkmenistan—

It's complicated says the Indian—Ashoka
maintained armies, it wasn't pleasant
A Dodge Charger like cavalry plowing
into counterprotestors—confront your enemies

Within and without—or was that Freud
shut off the TV power down the computer
in hand in head, sleep comes easily when it does
sunlight this morning in our garden

The clipped grass manicured azaleas
and avocado pear coneflowers and orchids
summer cypresses greener than your God
Ganesh the cicadas wouldn't stop
chattering above roaring cars above
thundering jets a thousand year memory
of the waking dead and the dispossessed

Accident South of Gainesville

Crickets enlisting cicadas trembling
body parts rattling Sunday morning
before cars come out—soon
driverless—above cheeps in bamboo
clusters—Solzhenitsyn unread twice

Who cares for life in a Soviet past
or Ryazan or a Russian district
school comrade! The politburo gone
to China and India—traffic halted
highway becoming parkway

We emerge from vehicles like cicadas
from a fifteen year slumber loitering
near guardrails twisted and broken
where lights flash where officers

Issue tickets and supervise removal
of bodies—what is one hour 15
minutes or 15 years to dead or living
dead, raingreened grass—the lake

Underlooking a Thai restaurant
green—fishermen paddling
flat-bottomed boats—noodles
in curried gravy mirroring reeds in water

And the rain-splashed highway shoulder
overgrown and flowered—a solar eclipse
tomorrow for four minutes day is night
sun in moon's shadow and summer dying

Indian Swastika

We laugh together Jew who would not
forgo a name like Letterman or a skull
cap quoting some ancient pact
with Abraham good until eternity
cutting off cockskin—god creating flawed
males—who hears wisdom at ninety-nine

We laugh together African singing
ebonics and jazz and blues is gospel
black like whip and unpaid labor
on southern plantations lynching Lee
on stone horses or dragons

We laugh together Hispanic—latino
outmoded—who will not give up bueno
or garbanzo—that pea from Asia
and avocado could never be pear

I who am neither white nor black—watch
my language—or Hispanic or of The Book

How could I be white nationalist
or Hindu with this Sanskrit Swastika
I cannot carry in public except
with an apology and an asterisk

Yet we laugh together lunch together

The Passing of Irma*

No banging on doors or rattling
windows no popping no roar
like an empty plastic barrel
dragged on a night road—and
still no silence only a quiet
weeping rain in place of your eye

---

*   Hurricane Irma

After the Storm

When we went to bed they were marching
on the city's white sections—not Twain's
land whispers Tom whitewashing a fence
stepping back to admire paint—sunshine
this morning cleaning up after Irma
wind's processions wearing masks. Not white
hoods. Red bandanas hiding dark faces
at midnight a woman gives a finger to cameras

What are in those backpacks—there are gun
toting boys says a reporter. This is not
unwrong. Hunting bombers in London—
Islamo-terrorists—no one uses the "I" word
not the city's Muslim mayor. We board up
storefronts windows before the storm—
wood fences blown down are back up, Frost—
good fences = good neighbours—barricades
we are all unwrong. MLK had a mistress
Valmiki was a highwayman—stones
and bottles already thrown at lawmen

In the hurricane's aftermath we search
for uniforms for reassurance—looters
come at night when dark has no colour

Correcting

Cultivated blooms ringing lawn
are wildflowers in Flatwoods
morning's sultry dawn fallen pines
touching trail after Hurricane
Irma is what kind of name—'morning

Two walkers hug, neon skirts merging
before mile marker 1 Hindu numeral
on Roman measure of distance—
the Emperor lives empire ghosting another

Dimension simultaneously physicists show
in formulae how ibis flocks overhead
in formation on a southern peninsula
and in Africa, India realtime—we do not know
in one hundred years, two—this is home

This is home. Will you return to Europe
rhetorical—General Robert E Lee
still marches leading ghost armies on stone
horses discoloured in neglect—pull them down

Pull them down at night in daylight Lenin
and Hussein toppled sideways—but will we
give up Empire's language and speak
Sanskrit or Swahili—wear loincloths and dhotis

New World Upanishad

Talking back to wind jamun leaves sway
we have passed the hurricane's eye
unbroken, bending backwards like acrobats
—trapeze artists from a subcontinent
to continents south and north—an Atlantic
peninsula refurbishing stale dreams

We no longer hear difference in swishing
branches in pinnate or complex leaves
or tide turning back on itself rolling sand
on sand—or rubber wheels assaulting asphalt
—once irritants—scents of unfamiliar foods
cured hams, curries from adjacent cubicles

We bend and snap but do not break—
this Indian Orchid's heart-leaves dense and
thousand twigged hiding scars of a thousand
years—cancer infecting marrow and mind isn't

All We Wanted

Monarchs flying unerringly north
of Toronto and back alighting on neem
a gnat-catcher diving—
I've lost my way I live on insects

Sentinel fowls warning West Nile
Virus is here—chickens as guinea pigs
wear long sleeves head indoors at dusk
admire sunsets within glass walls

Amazon is neither river nor warrior
in interiors' controlled air purchase the world
—but butterfly why have you come again
taunting us outdoors—kids once kids again

Sneaking up behind as you imbibe nectar
caught between thumb and forefinger
releasing pixie-wing-dust adhering to skin

Heading north that time like migrants
to Mexico vowing to demolish borders
Yogic or—yogi Paramahansa silent to critic
unbaited—I fly blindly you think
a thousand years or ten thousand kneed
with pen straying off course to see

Same things I've always seen known
celebrating July4th with starburst fireworks
no longer Asian gunpowder your women
tethered to sullen firesides planning on tables
crafted by men—new flesh on old bones

Waiting for your companion—prey or predator
is this all we ever wanted—respect or learning
and yearning sex orgasm O god yes yes yes
a porn starlet—but why how do butterflies mate

Sound

We had never heard this before
a tiny popping like water dripping
from low-hanging eves after rain
in a Florida fall November's dry leaves
mingling with stunted grass and Carolina
wrens—climate change another thing
moving from Toronto to Tampa
what once was cool now cold—last week's
leaning jamun twigs purple on top
green under leaves stringy like vine maple
and this we'd never heard before—
juvenile cardinal learning to tweet

Another Upanishad

Brown wrens in brown grass
one week's cold—morning frost
virgin cotton on the car's blue top
mirroring indigo sky—sunshine
and wrens flitting in and out
like delight, a ripe spice mango
we never remember never forget

Wales Estate, Wales Market

Almayer's Folly in memoirs
of cane cutters or women
weeding cane rows white
rumals cooling heads in sun
in shade grouped in circles
stooping in Friday Market

North of factory and cane-lifts
master and mistress, sweet crystals
conveyed overhead loading ships
in the Demerara sailing for Europe
or Canada, candies sweet teas sweet

Foods, diabetes—type 1 type 2 type
drafts on an old royal typewriter
ghosts of men of women—
Mira naming herself in songs
in poems to Krishna we still sing

Five hundred years later
O Rani O Rajput folly—take
that Dylan—Ikea "Swedish
for common sense"! or Nobel folly

Brown-skinned women's voices
twinkling above market roar payday
trips and sips from "flatties"
Demerara spirits heading north—
rums soaked in English oak casks

A retired General's vengeance
as Commander-in-Chief, President:
close these money-losing diabetes
factories, estates of my ancestral slavery
—but, really, let's punish the "coolies"
who took their places who prospered—

Rain: we ride up the rumshop
ramp sheltering on the raised wrap
around verandah with estate women

Squatting, frock hems looping
between legs—no fat in sight
chatter and laughter erasing rain
and overcast—*want a sip schoolboy?*

South American Scotch—laughter
—El Dorado coloured rum and you
can hear their sugarcane ragas
if you listen carefully to Sase's folly

Coffee and Tea

We are your servants colonialist
languages we speak and defend
a sneeze—salud! Roll your tongue
roll your eyes at chip cheep tweet
at morning and earth ribboned

With asphalt and wheels: rubber
and polyester steel belts, radial
this history coming around again

You say it wrong! This is how
you say: Puerto Rico and Bogota
in Espanol. Do you know lorry's
bonnet! You curse King George

Red winter coats are in fashion—
the English the Spanish the French—
Vive le Quebec!—blue skies
across the Atlantic facing Mexico

Or Mehico! You do not laugh
spreading ancestral tongues wide
as a kiss: Aztec Maya Inca
hahaha—dravidian from South

America—you know, Guyana
flying no flags but a Jhanda
occasionally red or white or black
tea—Darjeeling—predating The Raj

Pure Colombian beans. I don't drink tea.
No? How you say? Only coffee!
pure mountain Colombian, ah!
But what is chai, chai? Do I say right?

Yes, we say right in languages from Europe
blue skies white skies flags coffee tea chai

Christmas Postcard

May that grey wispy cloud
outside our door blow away
in this dawn condensation
on glass doors dew-drip
commingling with cardinal's calls
red slash in green palms
outside our portal we almost hear
fowlcocks crowing—rhode island's
red feathers—snow on straw lawns

Nila kantha clouds gone
in sindoor sunshine robillini
fronds swaying like Clara
Coconut trees—may you not recall
hairless head or chemo or cancers
but laughter from Colombia from
Amazon parrots chatter, Rudolph—
no red-nosed reindeer—tossing one
Ting-a-ling-a-ling ling-a-ting-a-ting
cork-lined metal caps and bottle
opener rattling El Dorado bottle
and XM Gold Raleigh couldn't find
in Guiana or Ponce a fountain

In Florida a scent of casareep—
ole man paapi thief fowl egg ole man—
Cockroach-Roachy, an Indian calypsonian:
drink-a-rum on a Christmas morning
drink-a-rum, Mama drink if you drinking
drink-a-rum on a—and later—*Mamas*
drink if you drinking—ibis squealing
like pigs arcing this morning's sky

Cars traversing Dennis Street—dust—
Drysdale and Tetley Streets and Teddy
—chacha*—barber brother father husband
not quite the only Indian living
in the ole "*nigger yard*"—unlike Carter
using no quotations to sanitize history—
sun in eyes and Teddy's pepperpot
smelling to Campbellville and back
to Ozone Park or—haha—somewhere
Behind Gad back in NY casareep
from Carib or Arawak or a Kaseek's gift
black cassava juice—sun in our eyes
how can we see colonialists we've become

"All religions are the same" a missionary's
slick lie or an atheist's facing east a Hindu
orthodox system we celebrate the Carvak—
"There is no other way, no other world
but this"—brothers, may we meet again
where kiskadees accost morning noon night
where jamun leaves sing and coconuts dance

We didn't come into this world alone
what names mingling with bodily fluids
not quite Kumar Jadoo Sourgh Shiv Ravi—
sun rising in east in eyes we cannot accept
Naam Samskaar** and every Jesus Jew
Siddhartha and every Ravi and Shiva
on mountain valley on plain on pastureland
in forest ardha—first half-man-half-woman
first yogi hay surya hay Bhagwan
Surya Namaskar an Asian in yogi tights

* Paternal uncle
** Hindu naming ceremony

Women performing on mats in Hickson
Park honed limbs oozing sex in a city
I would show Riverwalk instead of soup
kitchens a museum or two or four-headed
nila kantha—let this go you say
let my people go in celluloid obsession or—
we didn't know—propaganda—well, Roachy
still singing calypso and that old road gone
yet there in our heads: Dennis Street asphalted
pebble-embroiled tar paving over potholes
puddles but the Street's dust still in nostrils
until we sneeze or try that yoga breathing
exercise, kapal-bhati—you thinking West
Indianly battie or batty for buttocks—*bhai
you funny like-a-rass!* Hahaha—until we meet
again in sunshine storm or rain ting-a-ling-a-ling
ting-a-ling-a-ling—may there be peace
on earth and all that jazz or taan* or Kishore
Kumar or Mukesh**, our father singing eternally

*   A form of classical Indian singing brought to Guyana, Surinam, and the
West Indies by Indian indentured labourers
**   Kishore Kumar and Mukesh were famous Indian/Hindi playback singers

After Chichen Itza

Between frostbitten Florida leaves
and winter wrens are sun-shafts
heat's politics thumping cold
in the boisterous bamboo cluster
roars the same wind in the Indian
orchid's brown twigs rubbing
each other gaily like parakeets
en route to ancient Mayan centers—
a ball court where losers won
where winners were sacrificed
like fowl cocks in a Kali puja

Heat on our cold shoulders
until sundown, dust on our shoes
from last week's jaunt among ruins
in a forgotten land we know
pyramids by unknown builders

Brown Bird

Avocado-pear still rusting from frost
last month's jamun clutching toast
twigs Indian Orchid deleafed
baring limbs and chest like Gandhi

Still a warmer winter than normal
predicating a scorching summer
your cars your computers your smart
phones your paper waste activists
who did not plant the green azalea

Citrus laden with golden orbs
sourced on Mediterranean shores—
where Ovid is exiled from Rome—
or Formosa Azalea blooming
magenta lighting robillini palms
glinting in morning-shine hawthorn
overseeing rye-grass a trumpet
to day—who says earth is done
brown thrasher warbling nonstop
on a flight back north to summer

From Where We Be

We weren't where we said
we'd be dancing on ice
in some ancient college town
in the foothills of mountains
or terraced slopes holding paddies
or camellia sinensis rowed
foregrounding white-capped
Himalayas—if we come
to Niagara's thundering foam
winter-frozen water mid-sentence
no native chief no native thief
anchored in England or Scotland
somewhere in once-British Isles
singing I was born here after
decimating Calusas and Creeks
to Oklahoma alt narratives
from Germany mogul courts
Ithaca sending out Odysseus
in a fiction yolked elsewhere
I was born here Penelope—sun
and sand and hardwood groves
could we not be South American
Floridian—all immaterial
memory contradicting that uttered
in darkened rooms beyond
spinning fan-blades O love O loves
O loves we aren't where we said
we'd be in that century or this

Morning Tea

Birds infusing morning at sunup
overcast on plains mist rolling
in from sea the same moisture
floating down Himalayan peaks
Hay Shankara i and I and you and I
the same essence—only women
scan Darjeeling hillsides only women
plucking camellia sinensis bushes
—fingers brewing in my cup
head straps and backed baskets
balancing on terraced slopes
no snakes in shrubs no serpent
poised except in tasting rooms
exchanges and auction houses—
taking your pluckings first and second
and third and all your flushes
your fingers on tongue on morning I
and I advaita mountains on my plain

Palace

Wilson Harris 1921-2018

Nothing toping that peacock's palace
in the bush, a femur flute sounding somewhere
from Kaieteur's top, a drop unimaginable
except to interior surveyors. Topography.
Sightlines to London. Say what you will
about imperial measures. Drop to perpendicular
feet to yards—Europe's standardizations
like kilograms, or metres from Carroll's
instrument, Arawak bone teasing Donne
in white, ghosts on South American rivers
stone steps down this falls—nothing topping
space and time and sky except Mariella's
toes on Guyana marble—copper-gold treefall
divan thick—lush through Guiana forest
palace we shall roam a thousand years
like these greenheart pilings upholding
wharves in a hundred cities and ports—elsewhere

Darjeeling Royal: Beyond First Flush

Sun glinting off yellow-green oak
pollen and buds—but it is moon
in cup, hand plucked at purnima*
when oceans rise in estuaries
rivers in camellia sinensis bud tips
we are water falling in shower
Unashamed of blemishes flesh-folds

When you love you love even age spots
and fired leaves halting fermentation—
black tea—silver tips plucked at purnima
more precious by the pound than gold
for royalty not on Forbes' List—
who cares Scotsman what is on yours.
On ours, once, stars aligned in heavens
earth nearer moon tastable in first flush
fired lightly and golden green in cup

*   Full moon

Time Change

Landrover's whining in highland hills
green clothed courting calls from cashew
hued birds on weathered fences
board-on-board knot-holed, shrunken
in sun in heat in light pebbles beneath
asphalt potholes and great bamboos
swaying—take me home for your puja
wedding, everything upright falling down
tomorrow like water at Kaiteur's edge
frothy and forever rum-red today

Last year's summer flush or autumn notes
are Saraswati's veena plucked and dancing
down Darjeeling hillsides on Shiva's soles
tandav tandav tandav—me too you assert
me too—brisk and bold and meditative
enhancing hot tongues sucked in navels
everything in midday sun standing up
lies down wilts—please you utter drawing
blinds forgetting we're one hour behind

Ocean Voyages: Singing Taans from Kolkata

You who sailed down the Hooghly
into the Bay of Bengal passing
landowners—Thakurs anglicizing—
Rabi lost in contemplation on rivers
in Bangla country or from Chennai
bringing Madras curry, you who walked
on water for three months in tossed
barks on monster waves around
The Cape afraid to eat weevil rice
worm-ensconced daals—protein
is protein!—no tablets for nausea
for ocean-tossed jahajis, no lights
in holds on, or beneath, decks
only shining the twinkling from stars
a million light years—I am here
you are here in nau-graha or purnima
puja, full moon on unobstructed ocean
watching for birds, flotsam, moss
on indigo sea, you who said, chanted
will this bitching bark never land
in British Guiana and Chini-dad—
gold country and sugar-land—

Cruise-line cafeteria servers treating
Carnival kings and queens—food
24/7, no walks ten stories high
on a mini golf course, no thousand
ant crew scrubbing deck every night
and day no, no sir yes ma'am, no
wailing for who jumped overboard
unable to bear seasickness, land

yearning—we suck sweet citrus
like you Hanuman rising on water
bluer than indigo playing ball
on arc of sky—surya transitioning
to gulab jamun setting on water
O joy O land O land O land

Cowherds

Even without eyelid you see sloping rain
thrushes brown like soaked staves
you straddle—feathered horsemen—
we've placed no chemicals on our lawn
for foraging zebus, dappled longhorns
we watched from our mounts growing
plump with memories of chipped fields
or the milkman—Aja*—balding
one unflickering eye still twinkling
in time with tongue and laughter
riding a steam train like raja
scattering coins at stations until
his herd died—enemy sneaking in
buck-bead bush with evening fodder
the coconut plantation set aflame
buildings burning—arson—we didn't kill
our cows, Nandalal fluting ragas
milkmaids you think erotic minds
a thousand wives, bansuri at dawn at dusk
Gopis wandering into moonlit meadows
not ragas precipitating rain or firing forests
in Amazonia or Africa or Indonesia—
shanti filling udders and pails, buttermilk
chor you say—but did we mind cows
for footwear for milk-white pera for palates

---

*   Paternal grandfather

Red Bird on My Lawn

After "rain-like-peas" cardinals
pecking on this greening lawn
ending drought. We are Dalits
today. Meaning what philosophers?
We see the red coat first
then brown plucking ostentatiously
in harmony. Even knowing nothing
of ornithology, we stare, admire
sunrise and sunset and midday sun
on feathers. The Devil rules in Hades
if you're Greek or Italian—brown
I was unnoticed in school. Are you
gay, she asked. Everyone said—
because you didn't take me on
that midnight walk. Or even touch
limbs aflame vulva throbbing
Florida night stars dancing.

How ripe are red mangoes red coffee
berries from South American plains
or reggae mountain island rising
volcanoes once in memory, a flag
flown by Leninists after the purges—
you mean murders, neutralizing
Romanovs, every last decadent royalist
no language is colourless—
except in the dark going down
whisper tongue: I practice yoga
I am vegan—tomorrow the butcher
is my hero, Lenin in Indian jungles—
your grass-knife tweets at my throat

Potted Gardenia

Mist-white resting in boot-polish green
singing dvaita-advaita take me
as you will—if you can wait
for evening when I draw nude limbs
if you can wait for morning's unfurling
perfume like none. No English rose
or French. Give me this southern moist
earth on limbs—this unforgiving sun

Mattress Makers*

We were picking red coconut husk fibres
sticking through new mattresses, cheapest
beds! we couldn't analyze in Port-of-Spain
or Oxford. Babu! The Pakistani wife—
Indian really—to shouts and protestations
recalling forgotten ancestries. Rain-rich,
this evening's velvet green cypresses
and bahia making everything grass-tinged
even slow moving clouds soon to weep
and rise higher, but this Mockingbird

Bed maker in Wiltshire or some such
countryside; the wheelchair motorized
brown fingers knowing where to pull
and push needle where to stitch—analysis
of fibres hued like Scottish hair—Erik
the Red's raiders seeding pockets of isles

Not coconut trees, yellow marigolds, buttons
on the lawn's lapels. These were our best
nights; not backs on steel and memory
foam but backs of steel. A hand patting
a hand pulling husk-dust from nariyal**
palm we scent a second coming

* V.S. Naipaul in his 2008 book, *A Writer's People*, describes a mattress maker
making coconut-fibre mattresses for his maternal grandmother in Port-of-
Spain. Naipaul's writes of this Indian man (born in India and who only knew
Hindi, a relative of his grandmother) in his usual acerbic tone tempered with
an empathy reminiscent of his great, early story, "B. Wordsworth." That image
stayed with me for several months, sparking my own memories, as a boy, sleep-
ing on similar coconut-fibre mattresses—later made and sold by reputable
mattress stores in Georgetown. My first draft of this poem was on May 17,
2018, three months before Naipaul died—confined to a wheelchair in the
months before his death
** From Hindi—coconut

thinking of some calling for a hundred
thousand words—three dozen books
unimportant to shipwrecked mattress makers
on islands in the Atlantic—not Crusoe
on Barbados. We do not dream of India
in a Guiana* or English countryside
just needles stitching a handful of dust

Hoping souls find peace, Om Shanti, Shanti, Om

Rain

Squirrel watching from bone-bleached paling
rotting below golden marigolds new-minted
coins bordering flushed lawn
cypresses still as murtis in morning drizzle
cloud-dome hiding sun thick as imagination
in a lightless night—everything ages
except liquid falling from sky from eves
overflowing rain gutters in a sudden squall
water recycled yet new in every drop and droplet

---

*   Guiana, or British Guiana, the Pre-independence name for Guyana

Sugarcane's Black Snow

White crystals slide like diamonds
into tea and dark-roast coffee
fudge after dinner and chocolates
sweet wine a memory chasing
black wisps from sharp cane-stalks
pre-harvesting burn wicking excess
moisture razor leaves and vermin—
if snakes could laugh fleeing
to air-conditioned offices avoiding
black ash in nostrils in lungs

We close doors windows unescaping
smudges on apparel buildings and lives
a cough's origin unnamed—Massa
day done and yet ash everywhere
harvests and profits and Selvon's line
like razor grass: "Cane is Bitter"
blood-sugar and diabetes coming later

Watch My Language and Yoga on

For one day, let us be within
and without emergency sirens
and needs to unmake urges—how
to spend wisely, to speak guardedly
today I will capitalize like a President
or not and the trolls will laugh
grammar invented by a "Brahmin"-Panini
I am a dalit, untouchable, lowest
of that Portuguese word you cannot write
—for one day let us be without capitals
and commas and trolls mocking
hahahahahahaha what is language for
if not for communicating first and last
always what we think. For one day
palatable fictions to a thousand pages
or a thousand fictions piecemeal
like birds on the fading paling—
thousand arms and thousand names
O Vishnu, O Krishna today without flute
or bow, day fading into dusk
and nothingness and a colourless rain
on wet wood ringing a sodden lawn
and big-bellied ponds and lakes, one day
without flooden—is this even a word—
roads, one day within and without caste
and keepers of languages we gave up
crossing sea and ocean from India
to South America, three months sailing
without kobo or TV, three months within
and without water and evening birds calling
watch your t, watch your I and yoga on

Taan* of Our Taans

Children or grandchildren—an outpost
in Trinidad—mountains and mileposts
where are we now? Lost among 17 million
in New York, back-home stores on Liberty
Avenue bought out by Chinese still selling
bora and seim, Guandong made murtis—
representations of Shiva Lakshmi Durga
with Mongoloid cheekbones cheaper
than Kolkata artisans'. Priceline isn't all
that matters. Thrush in late-blooming
citrus grove rakes morning quiet
like a madman with an AR-15
the only casualty is lazy Sunday—
lawn already cut—You-tube extending
into hours—drunkard on El Dorado rum
someone posting old album jackets online
scratchy audios of bhajans and taans
who the dholak player who the dantalist
long dead—Sudama the most enthralling
music from your Caribbean by way of UP

What! You crazy, man, mon, Indian—

I know your Marley your Mighty Sparrow your
Calypso Rose *and* my Sundar Popo—do you hear
or seal your ears like Floridians ensconced
in double-paned glass windows walls doors
everything even dampers in air conditioners
vibrating loose fins and gills not drowning
mockingbird and thrush and neighbours'
scorn of my skin—curry face masala scents

* Taan – A type of classical singing and music brought by Indian indentured
labourers to Guyana, Surinam, and the West Indies.

Smoke rising from my patio not barbecue
cattle carcass—cow's droppings repourposed
in agarbati with jasmine and attar petals—
sticks of incense distraction you think
non-conformity to Chinese fourth fireworks
exploding a sixteen-year-old's chest—dead

You hear and not hear egrets in my songs
morning thrush bold as Assam tea ibis gliding
down from cypress tops hawk on lamppost
waiting to pounce—old black and white pictures
blurry and imprecise taan artistes and renditions
online you will and will not know again bhajans
in raagic mode—a grackle piping redwing

I do not know I do not know—and neither do you
Afro-Euroists how blessed we have been—aye—
pedigree pouring out fingers on pages in epics

Memoriam for V.S.N.

Voices sputtering like lawn mowers
on overgrown summer lawn—you battered
an Argentine mistress; for twenty years flying
in for romps in Africa, journeys among
unbelievers, perhaps, a turn in the south

Whores in London. We are humans
too. Lahore Journalist having the last bite
and laugh. Before the moon goes down
before ashes scattered negotiations
for tell-alls, as if any one can tell all

Laughing from beyond at nephews and nieces
"My Uncle V." White lovers. How will you
repay ancestors if only the university
can think, analyze the sound of cars

In morning commutes and crows calls
like cats from wetlands or coins rolling
from slot machines and jay-screams telling
only what you know: the feline dead the guest

Whose room you opened for the roaming cat
spilling slowly laughing at vanity. Evelyn,
not a woman, promoting Oxford: unquiet English
in Guiana or Mexico or Kenya, Corfu or India

For all its ugliness and mystique, how many ways
to make roti—you could say whisky or gin
taking the edge off mornings and evenings'
acerbic tongues. All these hours at our desks

Offering their weight around waists
and bank accounts—unless you believe
in yoga in Krishnas and Arjunas who can halt
ages aging and old and young uncaring

For correctness except at mass shootings
close to home the bushy tailed rodent
hopping along fence runners—a holiday
and open season—you will be risen

Like bread dough twice again and fired
in a tandoor—a writer must be fit to write
to think through fogs, English mists
and cold and damp—in fiction you're God

Only so many times creating mainly dust and dirt
and darkness and dictators and yourself
transposed, your handful of dust quoting
Jagan's vanity and the "kabaka"—ruler-for-life—

In Georgetown did you ever see Chedi
in action, humbled—ahir, cow-minder progeny
like Krishna in jail. Kamsa is everywhere
and that flute's miracles—there is no good

Way to say: we celebrate your accomplishments
despising the person, untrusting the teller

Seven Minutes: Jamal Khashoggi

Still you trusted king and kingdom
the black prince—in Florida too
we look over shoulders for assassins
Saudi oil in pick-up trucks—road
rage—who scrubbed the consulate walls

Leaving two phones with intended outside

Still you trusted king for divorce documents
ancient ruler taking three wives—ah India
guardian of the black stone lingum or not
—come into my house said spider to fly
more spiders arriving with knives bone-saws

You will walk in but never walk out.
Flinging body on study table, screams
heard downstairs and in Turkic spy mics

So you are writer! We sever fingers
first. You see. You feel. How say you
in Arabic. We look over shoulders too late

Celebrating holy days—neutralizing
animals gifting flesh to beggars. Choicest cuts
—halal, kosher—perfecting the art

Of dismemberment. Cameras show cleaners
and jugs of cleaning chemicals—an entire
crate. Just seven minutes said the butcher

I use headphones while I use the saw
music when Dumpty sits on a wall
singing "fake news"—the black prince

Will investigate. Cover all except your face
eyes names transcripts—we worship black stone
in swirls like bees in a swarming hive O Shiva

What did you do to Ganesha's head
What did you do to Ganesha's head

Parrot

For Peter

Returning to Greece, Alexander brought a bird
"speaking an Indian language"—Aristotle recording
in animal history and Ctesias notes—for a thousand

Years Europe thinking parrots only came from India

You held that stick passing it back and forth Moira
Kololo Makerere Leeds—Yorkshire man Boycott
white buttoned down flannels driving elegantly

Through covers brown hands catching red
sphere stitched leather disrupted and willowed
to boundaries: raven, or was that crow, exulting

I have the longest memory—Ganesh elephant-headed—
I perch on ledges webbed on swamp-cypress limbs
I shall remember you to yourselves returning voices

Konkani—Jazz in Africa Armstrong blowing life breath
into adopted saxophone fingers and lips vibrating
prana and curiosity—opening that bag—no slumber

Odysseus, fire-engine sirens waking neighbourhood
disrupting old orders in a pandemic—I did I didn't
come from Wuhan I did not come from labs I did

Not come from pangolins—bat stroking sphere
gliding on clipped green to boundary not baseball
not cricket not tiger putting on grass or putting gas

Into endless tanks not wind in sails in Dutch blades
now metalled in China or Spain Don Quixote charging
I ride an ass I am Sancho faithful companion follower

Astride a donkey I wear a thorn crown
plasma leaking unto forehead into eyes—what
has been as simple as a falcon's dive lord

Of birds fastest terrestrial creature clocking 242 mph
not kilometers but Roman measure not cheetah's
burst on savannah bringing down wildebeest or deer

Big cat brave-hearted lion—singha—leaping
to East Africa or Southeastern Asia Malaysia Singa-
pore's neither man nor beast Merlion crossing oceans

Ulysses Sanskritized Irish English words running
unto another word another line page breath, Bharat's
ancient treatise on dance music rhythm in mouth feet

Shiva unlost in Kampala heads feeding fishes—what!
we haven't renamed a Lake Victoria—imperial
utterance we brandish with love grain-hoarder-Caliban

White-crowned George rising at York—"my hair
is grey, but not with years, nor grew it white
in a single night"—*ah O twist karay dam da da*

Da da da dam, ah O twist karay—Junglee Kapoor
in Mumbai imitating Elvis vinyl spinning areas
of darkness engulfing America—watch your part

Of speech your tense your dissent your prepositions
odd in New England snow falling on Yale on Boston
harbour insurrection against old King George

China tea or Darjeeling's dumped overboard, native
tribes taking sides red-coated cardinal welcoming
dawn on paling blue jay screaming—you still hold

Colonial colours—republican red mimicry British military
blue democrat a default French smarting Drake's
victories or Hawkins'—blue privateers blue Fleur-de-lis

Fluttering in Florida on Quebecois antennas Atlantic
waters down middle passages tending to equinoxes
Japanese by spring another trickster from Africa

Spiders inhabiting landmasses in trickster traditions
the land is everything—story and character—Geronimo
finally subdued transported two thousand miles

To St Augustine to a Spanish citadel unvanquished
vanquished in a dark cell converted to Christ
ocean roaring in ears far from Chihuahua-Sonora sands

Straddling what U.S.-Mexican border ancestral grounds
unboundaried plains—Wounded Knee Little Big Horn
echoing over tall grass concealing bunting cougar peregrine

Falcon diving blood cardinal calls lighting dawn tweets
on Mediterranean fruit Florida-ized machine gunned beaking
woodpecker targeting dried Indian orchid bark—I bloom

Anywhere in the fall, give me a little cold or snow
Iowa or Alberta—how did you arrive from Yale or London
Salvam Salwan Selvan Selvon or Nazareth ancestral

Name in Goan gumbo garam masala Mississippi masala
Kampala masala Amin up general up moon up

Your time up Indian—no, not you with no name
no fleecing Indian name—keeping my finances under
poetry under Eliot or some biblical passage clothed

In a brown mantle Islam or Judaism still people
of the book not Patels or Bengali babus Bhagchee
Mukherjee Dutt Blaze Narayan Narayan Narayan

Narareth a brown thrasher skimming hedge beyond fence
a spring arrivant Holi-splashed African orchids blooming
somewhere in Moira—Prabhu a Konkani gift my name

In banana fronds in beaks of birds keepers and markers
of land and music notating a Rigveda or Yajurveda's verse
only bird "uttering human speech"—songs parrot ragas

When I Go

Wind in cold bamboo rustling morning
a walker's dog beyond fence half-growling
blue jays quarreling with day. Toronto
no longer "the good"—shootings in Jane-Finch
another on Danforth. We slither down
the Don a slow snaking vehicular train
new towers sprouting like weeds
in a Tampa lawn blocking out the CN tower.

Fall comes late to Florida—"hard-ears" state
always "a gentle soul passing"—kind-hearted
pioneering wisdom! But when I go mark that
schoolboy kiss—indiscretions touching a virgin's
vulva—the passion of a slap in Patentia—what
kind of name is that? Misplaced prepositions.

Today I write like a Raj. King without kingdom
but when I go don't forget youth's fire
the day I thought, "Daddy, you fool!" ready
to fight ancestry, birth, birthright
giving no quarter, no good and simple quote
for epitaph—yet remember no stone
on my head no marker but fire raging
in the forest of mind and fingers
no longer clutching fingers—this morning
the honey wren swallows a juvenile lizard

Raga for a New Year

May wrens forage in our yards
sing from rafters and rooftops
may doves nestle in our grass
and neighbourhood canines
and cats—stalkers—stay away
"Good fences make good . . . "
may woodpeckers feast on our
wood-rot tapping rhythmically
like woodpeckers—yes, may
we laugh at ourselves—and
the Trades blow where we're
headed across continents and
rivers and oceans—there is only
one ocean you quip—may sun
balance precipitation dissipating
ancient aches and memories—
windmills windmills windmills
may songbirds always sing
on our palms on oaks on senses

Finding Rembrandt

Rough marks from back to front missed
by ordinary eyes. Not intuition, not heart.
Evening soul when ibis flocks frolic
twittering in dusk and night candles
illuminating dark paint. This same canvas
living differently under midday sun

Gold in early night sky a gilt edged frame—
a noise invading soul, father, something
we waited on like butlers. When will sun set?
When will stars ignite space picking your
mandolin strings, evening ragas and teenage

Rebellions behind—you mean like Six
or that Spanish Seis passing for Sase from
some misplaced Sanskrit noun, or Dutch name,
Demerary devolved in Demerara—a river, sugar

Rum, a South American Dutch colony giving
us life, and merchants and painters waiting,
waiting. When will these blues arrive from India?
dark indigo sky—no shadows in light
but in shade, in negative spaces, in lace collar

Alone at Vreed-en-Hoop stelling after Devi left
sun descending on river, on ocean, on void heart
and yet this fullness finding self; art is art
is obsession, we said, there is no money in poetry

Holi: Spring Festival of Colours

May there always be spring in our eyes
and fingers, feet: pink ixoras, red hibiscus
mauve madar—green buds everywhere

Even live oaks' allergenic dust coating everything
yellow, golden—gainda, daddy said, not marigolds
pani re pani tera rang kaisa—is it rain—or

Water what is your colour? Or plucked stings
Mukesh mixing easily with jhaals chiming
from UP: Holi Khele Raghuvira Awadh Mein

May we sing for a thousand years—more—
chowtals, olaras—Mamas crafting coconut gojias
dholaks in arteries, hearts, ancestry's souls season

Sasenarine Persaud is a Guyana-born Canadian American author of Indian ancestry and originator of the term "Yogic Realism." He has published essays in *Critical Practice* (New Delhi), *World Literature Today* (Oklahoma), and *Brick* (Toronto) on this subject. His lifelong engagement with Indian philosophies, art, and languages and an awareness of his community's 184 years domicile in the Americas, clearly distinguishes his craft.

Persaud is the author of 15 books of prose and poetry, including *Canada Geese and Apple Chatney* (stories), the title story of which is anthologized on both sides of the Atlantic and included in *The Oxford Book of Caribbean Short Stories*, *An Anthology of Colonial and Postcolonial Short Fiction*, and the *Journey Prize Anthology: Short Fiction from the Best of Canada's New Writers*; two ground-breaking novels, *Dear Death* and *The Ghost of Bellow's Man*, and his signature, raga-infused poetry collection, *A Surf of Sparrows' Songs*, which alternates between Miami, Toronto, Guyana's Atlantic coast and India. His poetry has appeared in several anthologies including *The Oxford Book of Caribbean Verse*.